S.P. SUARKER

E-Commerce Business

The Essential Guide to E-Commerce Success, Learn All the Valuable Information You Need in Starting A Successful E-Commerce Business

Descrierea CIP a Bibliotecii Naționale a României
S.P. SUARKER
    E-Commerce Business. The Essential Guide to E-Commerce
Success, Learn All the Valuable Information You Need in
Starting A Successful E-Commerce Business / S.P. Suarker. –
Bucharest: Editura My Ebook, 2020
    ISBN 978-606-983-597-5

S.P. SUARKER

E-Commerce Business

**The Essential Guide to E-Commerce Success,
Learn All the Valuable Information You Need in
Starting A Successful E-Commerce Business**

My Ebook Publishing House
Bucharest, 2020

CONTENTS

CHAPTER 1

WHAT IS ECOMMERCE AND WHY YOU
SHOULD TAKE NOTICE

If you're looking to make money online, or even if you just want to increase the profits of your existing business; creating an ecommerce store is an excellent strategy. Scratch that: this is 100% the best way to make money online *and* that goes for hobbyists, entrepreneurs, bloggers and small businesses alike.

Bold claim? Sure is! But read on to find out why we can be confident in making it.

So just what is ecommerce? Of course the term refers to online commerce: i.e. selling products online.

But while ecommerce *could* mean selling an ebook from a landing page, it is most often used to refer more exclusively to online shops that sell multiple products and that have a particular layout and set-up. The most popular example of an 'ecommerce store' is undoubtedly Amazon. This acts just like a high street store and allows you to browse products at your leisure and add them to a shopping cart. The only difference is that you can do all this from the comfort of your home and once you check out, the products are the simply delivered to you wherever you are.

It's a familiar concept, but what makes it so important?

Why Ecommerce is the Future

Why Ecommerce is the Future

#1 Ecommerce is Growing

The first thing you need to recognize is that ecommerce is growing. In the early days, people were uncertain about spending money online and found that it was daunting handing over their card details and trusting in a supplier that they couldn't meet face to face.

But now look at companies like Amazon and eBay. These are household names around the world and everyone from the young and tech savvy to the elderly are now happy to shop with them. These companies have helped many people to put aside any concerns they might have had regarding ecommerce and to trust in buying online.

And ecommerce is growing as well doing massive business.

For proof, you need look no further than stats from 'Cyber Monday'. Cyber Monday is a national holiday of sorts where online retailers are anticipated to lower their prices. It follows Black Friday but these days it tends to do nearly as much business – and it's growing *rapidly*.

For example, in 2014 Cyber Monday created a total of $2.59 *billion* sales online. That's no small number but in 2015 this was increased to $3.19 billion. That's a huge increase. $2.28 billion of these were on desktop (versus $2.04 billion last year) while $838 million were through mobile devices (versus $548 million).

Across all devices, Cyber Monday increased by 21% from last year!

Seeing as Amazon is probably the best known online retailer, how is its growth going? Well, the company sold a total of $107.01 billion worth of products in 2015. The company employees 230,800 and there are 304 million active Amazon customer accounts. The brand is worth $47.73 billion and this is only expected to continue to grow as well.

The story is the same across the board. People are becoming more and more familiar with ecommerce and highstreet stores are struggling. This is undoubtedly the future of selling and it's easy to see why.

#2 It's Convenient

So what is it that has led to such growth in ecommerce? Well, the simple fact of the matter is that online sales benefit everyone. The only reason online sales haven't *already* dwarfed physical sales is probably the fact that some people still don't trust shopping online or aren't sure how to go about it. Over time this concern will be eroded more and more – while tools like PayPal will make it easier and safer than ever before.

When you sell products online, it means that you don't have to employ staff and you don't have to rent the same amount of physical space. You'll need somewhere to store your products (unless you're drop shipping) but other than that, your only costs will be hosting, shipping and web design.

Lower overheads mean more profit for you but they also mean lower prices for customers. Customers now have the ability to order products online conveniently but on top of that, they'll be getting them for a much lower price.

There's also greater versatility in terms of what you can sell. With an ecommerce store you can sell physical products which will require some up-front investment. But

There's also a lot less *up-front* cost. If you wanted to set up a highstreet store, then you would need to be willing to spend a large amount of money to rent the physical space, to invest in the stock and to manage staff etc.

However, if you are setting up an online store then all you're going to need is some inventory to sell (perhaps not if you are going to be selling digital products or acting as an affiliate) and a website. It takes just a few clicks to set up an ecommerce store and that means you can have one up and running in minutes for a negligible cost.

#3 It's the Best Way to Monetize a Website

The last two examples explain why businesses should launch their own ecommerce stores and why you might consider launching an ecommerce store *as* your business. But you should also sit up and take notice if you run a blog or website already and you're just looking for a way to monetize it.

Why? Because it's actually one of the most effective methods there is of making money from a website.

Until now, you likely have been relying on one of several methods to make money online. Perhaps you're making ads from advertising on your website (Google AdSense for example) or maybe you're making money by selling an affiliate product.

In either of those scenarios, it's important to recognize that you have placed yourself at the bottom of the 'foodchain'. In other words, you're being paid by those advertisers and product creators in order to send business their way. The fact that they're happy to continue paying you, means that they're making more money that that from you. In other words, they're earning more from your visitors than you are! You're getting a small share of *their* profit but they're taking home the lion's share. And in fact, you're essentially doing their work for them!

And that's why you'll typically earn about 1-50cents per click on an advert. Meaning in turn that you're going to need hundreds of thousands of visitors to your site a day to make any reasonable money. Compare this with selling your own products and making $20-50 ach time. Of course it's much easier to get someone to click on an advert than it is to get them to buy something – but not as much easier as you think if you have decent products and you're running your store well. The bottom line? You can make a living from a website with just a few *hundred* daily visitors instead.

If you have an ecommerce store, then the buck stops with you. Now you're making the maximum profit from your customers because you're selling something to them and keeping the difference. What's more, is that you're keeping your visitors on your site and engaged with your brand. You're not sending them away, you're keeping them right where you want them and making a real difference to the way they see you.

Finally, selling ecommerce products is better than selling digital products or affiliate products because it's something that anyone can appreciate. Only a very specific type of person buys ebooks about making money online. Phone cases and clothes though? That has a *much* broader appeal!

Try putting an ecommerce store on your existing website and just *see* what a difference it makes to your profits. And the potential for growth is MASSIVE.

What You'll Learn

What You'll Learn

So with all that in mind then, it's definitely worth learning how to create an ecommerce store so that you can start maximizing your online earnings. And potentially, so that you can turn your small website into your very own global brand selling products that get you really excited!

That's where this book comes in. Here, you will learn:

How to run an online store and create an effective business model

➢ How to set up your own online store with one of several ecommerce platforms

➢ How to find, create or buy products you can sell online

➢ How to build a website and social media presence to promote your store

➢ How to stock and design your store to maximize sales

➢ How to price your products

➢ How to choose products that will sell well

➢ How to use apps, plugins and more to get even more sales

➢ And much more!

In short, you'll learn how to create an ecommerce business or add ecommerce to your existing model in simple, easy steps. From there, you'll then be shown multiple ways you can increase your profits and turn that business into a huge success.

Are you ready? Let's start selling online!

CHAPTER 2

AN INTRODUCTION TO ECOMMERCE BUSINESS MODELS

Now you know why ecommerce is such a big deal and what makes it such a fantastic tool for making money online.

But the next question you need to answer is how you're going to make this work for *you*. Having an ecommerce store is great in theory but it's what you do with it that really counts! And as it happens, there's no 'right way' to run an ecommerce store.

This book is aimed at everyone from small business owners, to hobbyists who just want to run a store as a side project. The way that both types of seller goes about creating and running their business will of course vary, so find the relevant heading here that applies to you and see how you can fit an ecommerce store into your existing business…

For High Street Stores

If you already have a highstreet store, then the good news is that you're already in the perfect position to start taking full advantage of ecommerce. You already have inventory, you already have a niche and you probably already have a website.

Adding ecommerce is simply the next logical sense. By creating an online store, you can give your customers the ability to order your products online which will increase your turnover and also give you a much bigger potential audience. What's more is that you can use your physical store to promote your ecommerce store and vice versa.

It's important you do this correctly though. You'll need an ecommerce store that will automatically synchronize with your physical store so that the inventory is updated when products are bought online or in store. Ideally, you'll want to find a solution that lets you use your EPOS (electronic point of sale) to automatically update the stock with no work on your part.

As a Side Business

As a Side Business

If you are in work and you want to try setting up your own ecommerce store, then you'll be starting from scratch. The good news is that any income you add to your existing income will be 'extra' meaning that this can be a very 'small scale' business model and you won't need to worry about trying to run the business on a massive scale or making a fortune from day one.

With that in mind, you can identify a type of product you want to sell, create a website and a store and invest in a small amount of inventory. Or perhaps you even want to make your own products? Either way, you can then simply invest *more* money each time you sell off what you have while keeping a little extra for yourself.

You can also use an eBay store and social media to help your sales and possibly run a blog to handle content marketing.

For Bloggers and Marketers

If you're a blogger or marketer, then you might already have an audience and a platform from which to sell your products.

This is simply a matter of adding a store onto your existing business in that case and then promoting it to your email list, your visitors and anyone else that you can influence. This business will start with you identifying a type or product that fits into your niche and then choosing an ecommerce platform to suit your store. You might decide to also remove AdSense or affiliate products from your site in order to focus more attention on your own store for maximum profits.

Some Examples of Ecommerce
Business Models

Some Examples of Ecommerce Business Models

So those are some basic models for your ecommerce stores. The next question is how you might apply them in the real world. Here are some imaginary scenarios to help you visualize what this might look like…

Clothes Reseller

A very simple and easy business model if you're looking to make money from home as a side business, is to become a reseller. What this means is that you're buying stock and then simply reselling it for a little more.

To do that, you will normally be buying in wholesale. So let's say you choose to sell clothes from home, this might mean that you buy 100 shirts for $600 ($6 each) and then sell them off at $12 each. This is called 'keystone pricing' and it's a fairly standard pricing system for a lot of wholesalers and manufacturers. Even if you only sell half, you'll have broken even. Ideally though, you will aim to sell all of them, giving you $600 profit. You may choose to keep $400 of that and then reinvest $200 so that you can order $800 of stock next time for $1,600 turnover.

Over time your 'pot' will grow. This then allows you to invest some money into marketing (Google AdWords or Facebook Ads for instance) and to diversify your line with different types of shirt and other items of clothing.

But right from the word go you can start making money from your store by selling to friends and also by selling some of your stock on eBay. This is all much easier though if you also try to focus on a specific niche and give your store some kind of focus to set you apart. For example, you might sell shirts aimed at a particular demographic (plus sized women, entrepreneurs, gay men) or you might sell shirts that have all have something in common (they're easy to iron, they're light and cool, they're bright colors). With a something that sets you apart and helps you appeal to a particular audience, it's more likely your adverts, your social media posts and your listings will get noticed.

Blogger With Ebooks

As we'll see in more detail later in this book, you don't need to limit yourself to selling physical products. You can actually just as easily sell digital products like ebooks and even software through and ecommerce store.

So if you have a blog that is currently selling a single ebook from a sales page, you might consider branching out and selling multiple books from an online store. This way you'll look like a much bigger business and people will be able to browse what you have on offer at their leisure. This also means you can use things like special offers, deals and more to promote specific books and you can place adverts for your books around your site instead of using AdSense.

What's more is that you can even start using things like apps and plugins to sell your books in more inventive ways. You can embed your ecommerce store right into your Facebook page for example for more direct monetization of your social media efforts!

Where to Find Products to Sell

Where to Find Products to Sell

No matter what your business though, you're going to need something to sell. Here are some ways you can stock up a shop, even if you aren't fortunate enough to own your own manufacturing plant…

3D Printing

This is a surprisingly viable option these days. If you have a 3D printer, or if you're happy to use a website like Shaeways (www.shapeways.com) then you can sell plastic or metal objects with nothing more than a 3D model file. That might mean you sell phone cases, jewellery, ornaments or even toys!

Wholesale

As mentioned, you can sell products by finding wholesalers and buying in bulk. There are other ways you can be a reseller too – such as adding value yourself by packaging products nicely or just finding them very cheap somewhere.

Crafts

If you have a skill such as painting or making clothes, then there's no reason you can't turn that into a business and sell through your own online store. You may also want to try selling through Etsy.com though as well.

Digital Products

There's no reason you can't sell digital products from your site. This might be an online course, an ebook or a piece of software. There are no overheads and there's no delivery!

Affiliate Products

Affiliate products are products that you sell for a commission. Some digital affiliate products let you keep as much as 75% of the profits!

Dropshipping

Dropshipping is in many ways the ideal business model! This means you sell a product that you didn't create, except you're allowed to add your branding to the product so it looks like you did. What's more is that you don't have to worry about shipping yourself – that's also handled by the other company.

POD

POD stands for 'Print On Demand'. Often this term applies to publishing, meaning that you print books only when you sell them. Both Amazon and Lulu have great POD publishing options.

Likewise though, POD might mean printing t-shirts or printing logos onto mugs. T-shirt stores are big money online and they're super easy to set up!

Outsourcing

Finally, why not just outsource the creation of your product? This is easiest for digital products but it can work for all types of things!

CHAPTER 3

CREATING YOUR ONLINE STORE PART ONE – YOUR WEBSITE

So with all that in mind, the next thing to do is to start *building* an ecommerce store!

The good news is that this is fairly easy. To begin with, you're first going to want to create a general website if you don't have one already. This is not only going to be used to promote your ecommerce store but may also provide the backbone of your store itself by providing a way for people to easily access it and find your goods.

An Introduction to WordPress

An Introduction to WordPress

To create a website that will act as part of an ecommerce store, you're probably going to want to make something using WordPress.

WordPress is a 'content management system' (CMS) that makes it easy for you to build your site, customize the look and add, edit and remove content as you see fit. It can be likened to a blogging platform similar to something like Blogger or LiveJournal – but it's much more powerful than that and can be used to build entirely self-hosted websites.

What makes WordPress so amazing is just how easy it is to set up. This is a website that can be built as easily as creating a Facebook profile almost. This is practically a one-click installation but from there, it's incredibly powerful and can provide you with all the features you're likely to need.

And I don't mean that WordPress is 'as good' as the tools that professionals use – this *is* the tool that the vast majority of professionals use. Or to be more precise, 40% of websites and blogs on the net are powered by WordPress and that includes many of the biggest blogs on the web like Mashable, Forbes, BBC America, Sony and more.

What this means for you is that you have a simple way to build a website that can be just as successful as any of those. This is a tried and proven means to build a website and removes the need to worry about whether the underlying code of your site might be holding you back.

It's simply good business to choose WordPress and it doesn't *really* make much sense to choose anything else!

And as though all that wasn't enough to make WordPress by far the best choice, it's also important to consider the huge amount of support and extra features that WordPress offers. The simple fact that so many big websites are using WordPress means that there's a near-infinite supply of people who can help you with any technical difficulties you might be facing and there's just as many support forums, online guides and more as well.

WordPress is also endlessly customizable and upgradable due to the 'themes' and 'plugins'. Themes let you change the way that your site looks and is laid out with a simple installation. Meanwhile, plugins let you install additional features which can include all kinds of things like widgets for the sidebar, like comment sections and like entire *ecommerce stores* (this is the point at which your ears should be pricking up…). Many of the options we'll be looking at throughout this book require you to be using WordPress – so just don't even think about it!

Setting Up

Setting Up

So with that said, how do you build your WordPress site? The first thing you'll need is hosting. This of course means that you're paying for space on a server that will remain connected to the internet. In turn, that means that anyone with an internet connection will be able to find your website as long as they have the right address.

From there, you'll then also need a domain name, which is the address people will type into their browser in order to be directed *to* the hosting you're paying for.

Fortunately, most hosting providers also offer domain names, removing the need for you to find both separately. What's also good is that both hosting and a domain name are relatively affordable and shouldn't set you back more than $10 a month if that.

There are plenty of great hosting/domain name packages out there and to begin with, you won't need to worry too much about things like your bandwidth or your space – usually a fairly standard package will more than cover you until your site gains some *real* momentum. And once that happens, you won't need to worry about the cost of upgrading your service!

While there are lots of options to choose from, a good choice that will suit most purposes is BlueHost. If you don't want to spend time comparing hosting packages, then head over to BlueHost.com and sign up there.

Make sure that you choose a domain name that will be helpful when it comes to marketing your site. You need something that somewhat describes the nature of your business but avoid using obvious 'key phrases' in your title – Google has said that the best practice for businesses is to focus on creating a brand.

Installation

If you choose to go ahead with a BlueHost account, then your hosting package will come with something called 'cPanel'. This is basically a control panel that provides access to a lot of useful features that can help you get started with your website.

One of the best things included with cPanel is option to 'one click install' WordPress. That does exactly what it says it does, so log into your BlueHost account, choose 'one click install' and then choose 'WordPress'. You'll be walked through the process and really does take less than 2 minutes. The only tip to keep in mind is to expand the 'advanced settings' as this will let you enter a store name and a username and password for your WordPress account.

cPanel isn't unique to BlueHost either. A lot of other hosting companies also provide the same features and will make it similarly easy for you to set up WordPress with a single click.

Failing that, you might need to go through the installation manually. This is a very simple process too. It involves using an FTP program or your hosting account's file manager in order to upload the files you need. From there, you simply navigate to the installation page through your browser and follow the few simple steps.

You can find the WordPress files as well as all the steps you need to follow over at WordPress.com.

Note that it's also possible to set up a 'hosted' WordPress account. That means that you won't need your own hosting account or domain name because your blog will be stored at WordPress.com. This is a great option for building a free website if you're a hobbyist. For making money though, it's not something you should consider as it will make your business appear amateurish and it will limit many of the things you can do with it.

Themes and Set-Up

Now just point your browser at www.yoursite.com/wp-admin and enter the username and password you chose. You're now logged into your dashboard where you'll be able to add or edit content, change settings alter your theme, install plugins and more!

The first thing you'll want to do is to change some basic settings which will include the site's name and its 'tagline' (at the moment it says 'Just Another WordPress Site'). This is still a pretty generic looking site at this point though, which is where adding and editing your themes comes into play. Simply log into your dashboard and then select Appearance > Themes > Add New. You can then browse through themes (both free and paid) that can be installed to completely change the look and navigation of your website.

Failing that, you can alternatively look at another external site such as Theme Forest (www.themeforest.com). Here you can find some more premium themes which will cost more but will also be more unique, more professional and more professional looking.

To install plugins meanwhile, you just need to go to Plugins > Add New. There are again plenty you can choose from including both paid and free options. These can do some excellent things for you though, from pretty much handling your SEO for you, to adding comments or other interactive elements to your website. You can also find plugins that give you more customization options (changing your fonts for instance), that speed up your site and much more.

Have a play around and see what you can come up with. You'll find that it's fairly easy to build a completely unique and powerful website that looks just as professional as any of the big names we discussed earlier.

CHAPTER 4

CREATING YOUR ONLINE STORE PART
TWO – YOUR ECOMMERCE STORE
PLATFORM

Now you have the website, you just need to add the actual 'store' component to that.

And again, this is very easy thanks to tools that practically automate the process for you. The only downside is that there isn't as much of an 'obvious' choice when it comes to your ecommerce store. That is to say that no single ecommerce platform stands out in the way that WordPress does. That just means you need to think a little and pick the option that best suits your needs.

This section will help you to make that choice and then talk you through the process of getting set up.

The Top Ecommerce Platforms to Choose From

The Top Ecommerce Platforms to Choose From

Hosted Solutions

Remember in the last chapter when we said you had the option of a 'hosted' WordPress site (you should do, it was about

2 minutes ago…). Well, you also have the option of choosing either a hosted or self-hosted ecommerce platform.

And just to reiterate, a hosted ecommerce platform is one that will be stored on an external website other than your own. That means you'll create your store a little like you would add a profile to a social media site. It means less work for you but it also means you'll have a little less flexibility.

Hosted on the other hand means that you'll create your store by uploaded it to your server just like you uploaded WordPress to your server. Essentially this becomes a new website, or a part of your existing website.

Even once you make this decision, you'll have a fair few options to pick from. Here are some of the top hosted platforms:

Shopify

Shopify (http://www.shopify.com/) is by far one of the most popular ecommerce solutions around and is one that nearly everyone has heard of. Like WordPress, it comes with a huge amount of support, plugins and themes meaning that you can tailor it to your exact needs and meaning that there are plenty of ways you can boost your sales. Some of these plugins let you do powerful things like tracking your visitors and integrating email marketing, or like selling digital products and delivering them automatically.

It does lack some of the customization of hosted solutions however. For example, there's no option to create your own custom checkout page.

In terms of products, Shopify can support up to 5,000 different items, which is more than enough for most purposes. The basic Shopify membership is free but you might need to pay if you want to upgrade for more advanced features. Still, it's not prohibitive.

Bigcommerce

Bigcommerce (https://www.bigcommerce.com/) is hosted much like Shopify and is also suitable for up to 5,000 products. It's another solid choice but falls a little short of Shopify thanks to a higher price point. Moreover, Bigcommerce is less well-known than Shopify meaning that it doesn't have quite the same number of plugins or features. If you want to create a store that is in any way unusual, you should probably check first to make sure that Bigcommerce can support whatever it is that you're planning on doing.

Bigcommerce has one big advantage though and that's that it provides excellent support for international payments out of the box. This might be a big deal if you plan on selling to the US and the UK for example and don't know whether to display your prices in dollars or GBP.

Self-Hosted Solutions

Magento

Magento (http://www.magento.com/) is one of the best hosted solutions around in terms of its customization and features and is an excellent choice if you want to build something very unique with lots of power under the hood. This is the option that the big businesses with lots of money and tons of stock will want to use. If you have aspirations of taking on Amazon (you're mad), then Magento is the best non-custom-built option.

Magento supports up to 50,000 items and is installed independently from your WordPress site. The downside is that it's very fiddly and confusing if you're a new user. In other words, unless you have a good development team behind you or you're a developer yourself, you should probably stick with something easier at least to begin with.

And this is a point we should quickly make: when setting up your business always think about the 'path of least resistance'. Don't make extra work for yourself just because you want the pride of taking the less easy route – it's not good business. Focus on keeping your overheads (time and money) low and getting quickly to the point where you can reliably start making money. Don't let ego get in the way of good business sense!

WooCommerce

WooCommerce (http://www.woothemes.com/woocommerce/) is the self-hosted option that we would recommend. And what makes this such a great choice is that it is actually a WordPress theme. That means that you're not installing anything extra at all and the whole process of setting up is incredibly simple. You just install WooCommerce as you would do any other WordPress theme and from there, you'll have your store!

This does mean that your store is going to 'replace' the website you already had. This means you need to either consider this right from the start or you need to set up a secondary domain for your shop and then link the two together. Note that even if it does replace your site though, you can still have a blog on the store.

Like WordPress and like Shopify, WooCommerce has tons of support and an endless number of themes and plugins. This will make running your store significantly easier and makes it another great choice from a business perspective.

One limitation of WooCommerce though is that it can only stock 500 items max. This won't be a problem for most businesses starting out but if you have plans to expand it's something you certainly might want to consider.

Volusion

Volusion (http://www.volusion.com/) is a WordPress plugin but I's also somewhat unique in a number of ways. That's because it isn't *just* an ecommerce but is also an email autoresponder and more. Volusion lets you track our visitors and your leads and see who is looking at your products and who is reading your emails. Volusion is something that many internet marketer types might feel quite at home with but note that it's not particularly powerful or feature packed when compared with other ecommerce solutions and is really only suitable for small numbers of products.

Creating a Shopify Site

We're not going to go through every single ecommerce platform's set up process here. However, as Shopify and WooCommerce are probably the best hosted and self-hosted options respectively, it might be useful to look at at least these two platforms and how you get started.

Shopify offers a 14-day free trial which makes it easy to set up and start playing around and to decide if it's the right choice for you. To get started with that, head over to Shopify's site and then click '**Start Your Free Trial**'. From there, you'll be prompted to enter your email address, password and name you want for your store.

Click next and you'll be taken to a new page. Here you can add more details including your location and phone number for tax purposes.

On the next page you'll be prompted to 'tell [them] a little about yourself'. This involves answering a few questions such as whether you have a pre-existing store and whether you're running the store for a client or for your own business.

And with that, you're in! You'll next get to select form a number of store options. In settings you can change the name of the store and you'll also be able to start adding items to your store.

To start developing the store itself, click '**Add Online Store**'. You'll then be given the option to choose from several themes which work just like they do on WordPress. And just like WordPress, the themes can be both free and paid. Most of the more creative themes will be found in the theme store.

Click '**Customize Theme**' to alter the specifics of the themes and click '**Publish Theme**' once you're happy with it.

Browse to the next tab and you can select '**Navigation**'. This part is where you add individual pages and content. You can also choose to use either the current domain or to use your website's domain to make your store appear hosted (so it can be found at www.example.com/shop) for example.

Adding Products

To add products, just select '**Add Product**' from the front page. You'll then have to enter a title and choose an image that should help to sell your product. As you can imagine, the image is rather important to make your products as desirable as possible!

You will also be able to set elements such as the price and to add details such as a description. Of course you also need to add payment details if you want to start getting paid.

With all that done, your store is ready to go live! It really is that quick and easy to start selling and to start profiting in a big way potentially.

Adding Apps

If you want to add extra functionality to your site, then you can start adding apps as well which work just like WordPress plugins to enhance the features of your store. There are numerous apps that you can add to a Shopify store and you can find them by selecting '**Apps**' on the left hand side of the screen in the burger menu.

For example, if you want to sell digital products, then you can do this by using '**Digital Downloads**'. This app allows you to sell your products digitally and thereby make money from ebooks etc. without having to email them to your buyers.

Another great one is '**Pre-Order Manager**'. This does what it says and lets people pre-order your forthcoming products. The great thing about this is that you can use it to get people excited about your forthcoming products and to build buzz and it can even be a way to make sure there's a market for your product before you invest too much time into creating it.

And finally for this section, consider '**Recurring Orders**' by Boldapps. This app allows you to charge your customers on a recurring basis. This is excellent for selling your products on a regular basis – for instance if your customers want a monthly supply of protein shake, or if they want a subscription that will give them something new to read every week. Either way, recurring orders are very good for your cash flow as they provide you with a much more stable and predictable income and they convince your customers to potentially lay down more money for what you're selling up front.

Creating a WooCommerce Store

Creating a WooCommerce Store

Meanwhile, creating a WooCommerce store is even easier. All you need to do is to install WooCommerce via the WordPress 'plugins' store. Just search for 'WooCommerce' under **Plugins > Add New** and select it. Click 'Install Now' and then 'Activate'. You'll then be taken through some steps similar to those we looked at for Shopify. You can actually skip this to begin with though by just clicking 'Not right now'.

It's recommend that you *do* go through this process though so click 'Continue'. On page one, you'll be shown 'Page Setup'. This is where you can add the four pages that your site needs in order to operate. These are: 'Shop', 'Cart', 'Checkout' and 'My Account'. As you can see, each one is needed for the daily running of your site – but they operate just like any other page in on WordPress. Click 'Continue' to install them.

Next you will be asked to set up your store locale in order to choose your location. You can select a store currency too and set whether you want to use metric or imperial for showing the weight and dimensions of your packages. Note that if you want to, you can actually add a custom currency, though this may require a little technical knowhow.

Note also that you'll have the option to support multiple currencies later on via plugins. Select Continue and you'll then need to set up shipping and tax. You can choose your domestic and international flat rate shipping but you might not need to do this if you're going to be selling digital products.

You can import tax rates, or just skip this for later. Seelct 'Continue' again and then choose your payment gateway. A handy thing here is that you can use PayPal, which simply requires you to enter your PayPal address.

Finally, choose whether or not you want to let WooCommerce see your site diagnostic data. Once you've done that, you'll then have the option to create your first product, or to access other resources.

If you don't want to do that, then return to the WordPress dashboard and you'll find that it's rather changed with new options like 'Products' and 'WooCommerce' in your menu. The WooCommerce menu lets you see your orders, coupons, 'addons' (plugins) etc. Under products you can change settings or add new inventory.

For more tutorials and information, head here: https://support.woothemes.com/hc/en- us/categories/200152983-Video-Tutorials.

CHAPTER 5

DESIGNING A STORE THAT WILL SELL

Now you have your store, you're probably excited to start designing it and selling it! Creating websites using these kinds of tools is a lot of fun because all the technical stuff is done for you. All *you* need to worry about is choosing the themes you like the looks of, deciding what colors to use etc.

But don't get too carried away. While it's true that you can have a lot of fun here, remember that the end objective is to sell more items – and that means you need to think carefully about the layout and design of your site.

And specifically, you need to make sure that it is designed in a way that will encourage sales. This in turn comes down to a number of considerations and design choices.

Laying Out Your Store

Laying Out Your Store

If you were the manager of a highstreet store or a supermarket, then a big part of your job would be to decide how to layout all of the products in that store so that they would sell optimally. That means getting people to walk through specific aisles in order to find the best sellers, thereby being exposed to other products they might be interested in but hadn't considered for example.

In other words, the way you set out a brick and mortar store can end up having a big impact on the number of sales you make and this comes down to basic psychology. Of course there aren't quite as many factors for you to consider if you're going to be selling products online but there are still some ways you can influence the decisions of your buyers. Here are just a few things to keep in mind…

Security and 'Barrier to Sale'

One very important consideration for your store is the security and the 'barrier to sale'. Remember right at the start of this book, we discussed the growth of ecommerce and why it hadn't *already* grown to beyond brick and mortar store sales. The reason? People are concerned about spending money online.

If you want to sell to the broadest range of people possible, then you need to ensure that your site looks official and trustworthy. This is why it's so important to use a professional looking design and to create a professional looking brand with a high quality logo. Something as simple as a low resolution image, a typo or 'Copyright 2010' can make your website look less trustworthy and cause people to leave.

Another way to overcome this barrier to sale is to let people leave reviews on your store. This is something that many people will be nervous to do, seeing as it can potentially mean people end up leaving bad reviews! But overall, letting people leave reviews means that your customers can see *other* people have bought from you and received your products. If you respond to negative reviews, this will also reassure your customers that you're listening and that you care about what they have to say.

Easy Checkout

Another 'barrier to sale' is the time and effort involved in making a purchase. Believe it or not, this is actually a big deal and surveys show that people are much less likely to buy from a store if they need to set up an account first.

If you want to sell as much as possible then, you need to make the process of buying from you as streamlined and simple as possible. Amazon does this incredibly well with its 'Buy With One Click' system. But even if you were to mimic something like this for your site, your visitors might still be required to create an account the first time they shopped with you, which could mean having to input their card details, their delivery address etc. etc.

Again, try to make all this as simple as possible to make sure it isn't off-putting for your visitors. For example, one thing you can do is to use PayPal to handle your checkout process. This can help people feel more secure shopping with your site (as they don't have to input their details) *and* makes it a lot easier for them to buy from you.

POS

POS stands for 'Point of Sale' and is a concept that relates to the 'barrier to sale' we were just talking about.

In a highstreet store, you will often find something called a 'Point of Sale Display'. This is a display that will promote and sell a cheap product while people are waiting in the queue.

You've no doubt encountered these before and that's because they *work*.

The thing to understand, is that when someone has made the decision to buy from you, they will *already* have made that important psychological step that turns them into a prospective buyer. Prior to this point, they are still umming and ahing about whether they want to bother setting up and account or whether they want the guilt of spending money.

Once they're checking out then, they've already gone through the hard bit. Convincing someone to add something small to their order now then is actually relatively easy and means you can increase your profits further.

Of course you don't have a queue online, so your 'point of sale' is the checkout page. That's why you'll often find sites offering you to add extras to your order like gift wrapping for a small fee.

Color Scheme

On an unrelated note, you also need to think carefully about the color scheme and palette of your ecommerce site design.

What's key to understand here is that different colors can have different effects on your customers. For example, the colors red and orange actually make people feel slightly more impatient and have even been shown to elevate the heartrate. People find very red color schemes somewhat 'uncomfortable' and this can be used to your advantage.

For example, this is actually the reason that a lot of fast food joints are red or orange in their color scheme. The uncomfortable color palette means that people don't quite feel comfortable to spend a long time eating and this means that the store can accommodate a higher turnover of customers and make more profit as a result! And likewise, it turns out that if a 'buy now' button is red, it becomes more likely to be clicked more regularly!

Conversely though, if you want people to take their time and leisurely explore your site, then you need to make sure that you use cool and relaxing colors like blues.

Also important is to make sure that your color scheme allows you to use contrast. In other words, you need to avoid making your color palette too bright and your layout too busy. If you do that, then it will be impossible to draw attention to anything. Your aim is to make sure you can control the attention of your visitors and to get them to look at the products you're interested in selling. If everything is red and moving, then people won't know *where* they should be looking.

CHAPTER 6

MORE WAYS TO GENERATE MORE
SALES WITH PRICING AND PERSUASIVE
WRITING

More Ways to Generate More Sales With Pricing and Persuasive Writing

The design has a big impact on your ability to sell then but this is actually only one of the tricks you have up your sleeve. Also valuable is your ability to alter the pricing and to add smart descriptions to your store. This can not only make your items more affordable (and therefore increase the number of people who can and will spring the cash for them) but it can actually have a range of subtle psychological effects as well...

Pricing Strategies

Special Offers and Deals – Scarcity

A special offer is a great way to encourage more people to buy your products and if you price this offer correctly then the increase in turnover should help to increase your profits ultimately. In other words, you might lose out on each individual item but by selling *more* items you can still increase overall earnings.

But special offers and deals also have another effect – they introduce time pressure. People know that offers last only for a finite amount of time and thus, by introducing special offers and deals, you will automatically make people want to buy more quickly instead of going away to 'think about it'.

This in turn is very valuable for you. Why? Because people are most likely to buy things when they act impulsively. People buy most of the time based on emotion – *not* reason. So if you can get them to act quickly, they'll be much more likely to spend the cash than if you give them time to go away and mull it over. By using an incentive to act faster, you thereby make them more likely to act impulsively. And as such, they become more likely to buy from you.

Another way to make your audience act quicker is to make the products limited in stock. This creates 'scarcity' and doing that in turn also makes your items more valuable and thus desirable. People want things that no one else can have!

Contrast

We talked about color contrast earlier and making your products physically stand out on your digital shelf. But there's another type of contrast to consider too – and that's the contrast between your price points.

Whether we like it or not, our brains tend to automatically judge the value of something by comparing and contrasting it with other things. Something expensive only seems expensive (often) insofar as it is expensive *compared* to other things.

What this means is that you can easily make something look a lot more affordable by putting it *next* to something very expensive. And at the same time, doing this can also help make the expensive item seem more 'premium' and thereby luxury and desirable.

And furthermore, this means that you'll have more luck selling 'point of sale' options and upselling when the customer is already spending more. When someone is spending $500 on your website, they won't think much about adding $10 extra for a discounted product. But if they're only spending $5, then they'll be unlikely to want to add another $10 to the order.

Think about this when choosing what to upsell and how to utilize POS.

Bundling

Another option is to let your customers create their own 'bundles'. Bundling essentially means that your customers can choose precisely which items they want and which ones they don't need and thereby save money by buying in bulk but not end up with items they don't want.

Bundling is very effective because it ensures you have at least one option for every type of buyer. At the same time, it makes people feel as though they're getting a better deal while actually encouraging them to spend *more* in your store. It's a genuine win-win scenario.

High Ticket Items

When pricing your products, you might decide to include a 'high ticket' item that will land you a large amount of profit per sale. The aim is that just a couple of sales of this item will be enough to keep you in profit and in this regard, you might actually use your other products in order to encourage sales of those high ticket items.

For example, if you sell a lot of expensive products, consider adding something cheap so your customers can get used to shopping with you in a low-risk manner. This way you can overcome the barrier to sale, so that all you have left to do is encourage your visitors to spend the money on that product.

Persuasive Writing

Another thing that can make a big difference is the way you write the descriptions for your products. Here, your objective is to make sure that people act on impulse and are moved to spend the money right there and then rather than going away to think about it.

To that end, good persuasive writing for sales will need to focus on the emotional aspect of the product. And this means that you're going to emphasize the 'value proposition'.

A value proposition basically describes how a product will improve someone's life. In other words, don't just look at the sum of the parts but what people actually want to gain from spending the money. For example, people don't buy dumbbells because they need something heavy. People by dumbbells because they want to be strong, toned, healthy, attractive and confident. This is what you need to emphasize in your pitch because it will ensure that your prospective customers start imagining what life could be like after they purchase your item.

Meanwhile, try to get people to imagine what your product will be like to own (companies like Apple always use words like 'feel' and 'touch' a lot) and emphasize how quickly they can get their hands on it.

Split Testing

We've seen how color, layout and even wording can improve the effectiveness of your store and help you get more sales. If you get all this right, then you'll be improving your 'optimization' to increase 'conversions'.

But the question is how you know if everything you're doing is working. And to answer that question, you can use something called 'split testing'. This basically means creating two different listings for the same product, one using a red font (for example) and one using a blue font. You then observe how each listing performs over time and ultimately compare the results to see which design got the most sales. Once you have your answer, you adopt the winning change and this way you can evolve your site over time until it's perfectly optimized to convert the highest percentage of visitors possible into paying customers.

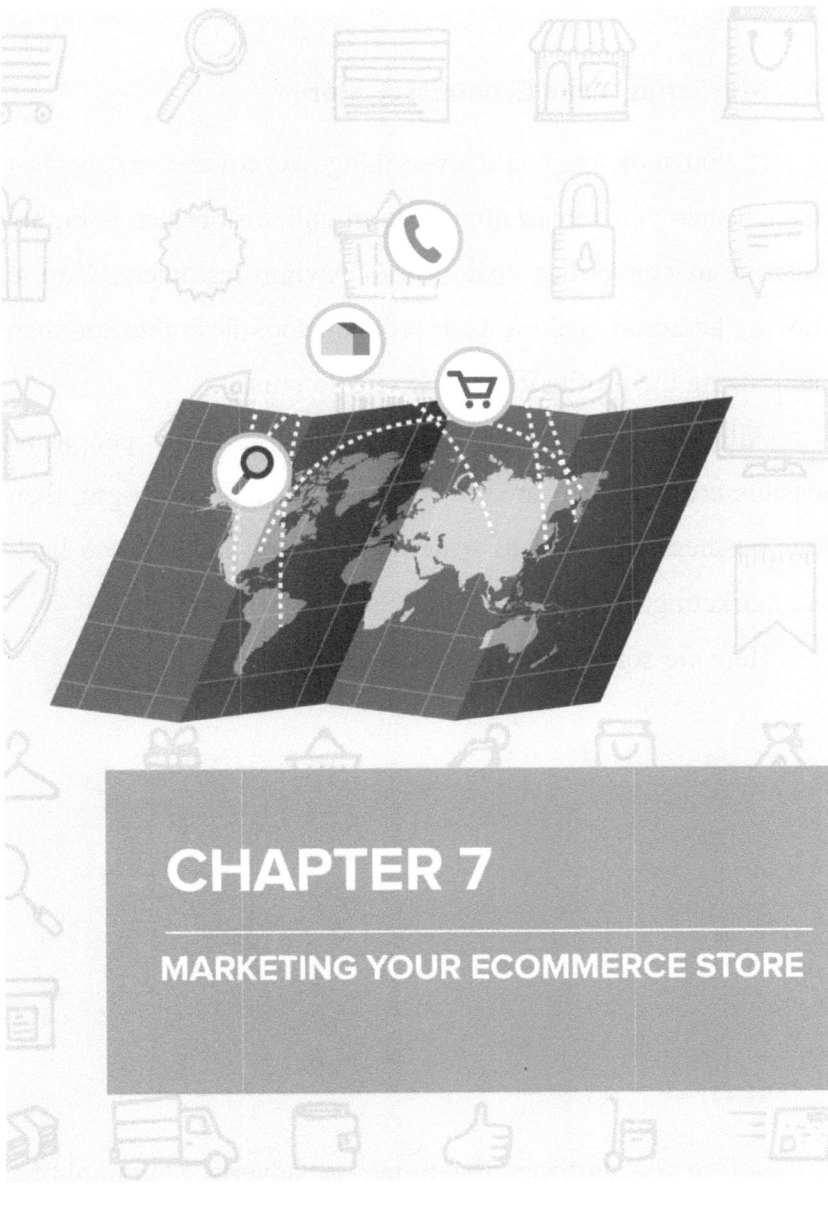

CHAPTER 7

MARKETING YOUR ECOMMERCE STORE

Marketing Your Ecommerce Store

If you took on board everything we covered in the last chapter, then you *should* now have an online store that is highly effective at converting visitors into paying customers. You're drawing attention, making your products look desirable and then maximizing the profits from each sale you make.

All that's left then is to make sure as many people as possible are *finding* your website. And if you do this right, then your business will start to scale and you can invest more back into marketing.

Here are some strategies you can use...

SEO

Before you start spending money on adverts, SEO might be a better first port of call. SEO stands for 'Search Engine

Optimization' and is essentially the process of optimizing a website and link strategy so that your store is easy to find on Google when people search for it.

To do this, you will often begin by identifying a search term (key phrase) such as 'buy hats online'. Only you won't want to choose 'buy hats online' because that will very competitive and very difficult to rank for. This is why it's such a good idea to have a particular target audience and a particular type of product. Remember how we discussed selling brightly colored shirts? Well 'brightly colored shirts' is likely a keyphrase that people look for but which isn't quite as competitive.

To start ranking for this term, you need to ensure you have a well optimized website (meaning it's fast, mobile friendly and easy to navigate) and that you include the keywords you've selected in your descriptions and on your blog occasionally. Aim for around 1% density, so for every 100 words, you can include the keyphrase once. It's also useful to include it in headers and in meta descriptions and then to try and build as many links as possible on relevant websites (that might mean getting a fashion blog to link to you for example). You might be able to do this by providing them with free content, which is called 'guest posting'.

Content Marketing

Speaking of content, content marketing is also a fantastic tool you can use. This basically means you're running a blog and the aim is to get people to subscribe and to look for your site when they want information relevant to your industry. So if you sell gardening tools, you should have an authoritative blog on gardening that peoples subscribe to.

In doing this, you'll now have an audience that trusts your recommendations and that listens to what you say. You can now recommend them your own products and even provide them with special offers.

Email marketing goes hand in hand with content marketing. Try to build the trust of your audience to the point where they're happy to hand over their contact details – then subtly sell your products to them.

Building an audience for your blog is of course the tricky part but you can do this by running a social media account and by using SEO.

Social Media

Speaking of social media, this can also be used to directly sell your products. One great way to do this is by promoting the value proposition and the lifestyle that your products support. So if you want people to buy your fitness books, this might mean running an Instagram account that includes lots of pictures of you training in the gym. You can also use 'influencer marketing' this way – why not get a big Instagram star to post a photo with one of your products?

You can even sell directly through several social media channels. Pinterest for instance now lets you sell straight through your account and so too does Facebook if you use the right WooCommerce plugin or Shopify plugin for your page.

Don't be afraid to ask your friends to share your page and your special offers either!

Note that with both content marketing and social media the main objective is to provide *value*. If you don't do that then people won't follow you and you won't have an audience to sell to!

PPC

PPC is 'Pay Per Click' marketing. This is an excellent tool for getting more sales but costs money. Basically, these platforms charge you only when someone clicks on an advert. This means that if the adverts don't work, then you won't be charged anything! You can set a maximum 'cost per click' though the more you're willing to spend, the more your advert will show up in competitive niches.

The biggest platforms for PPC are Googel AdWords (meaning your advert appears on Google) and Facebook ads. And they must work – Amazon spends up to $1M a day on AdWords!

And particularly useful is the 'remarketing feature' of AdWords that lets you advertise products that people have considered buying previously *back* to your old visitors when they're on other sites.

CHAPTER 8

CONCLUSION – STARTING YOUR ECOMMERCE BUSINESS

CONCLUSION – Starting Your Ecommerce Business

There's so much more to running a successful ecommerce business but a lot of it you will learn as you go. Hopefully though, you're feeling inspired enough now to jump in and start giving it a go. This is a fantastic way to earn money online and as we've seen, there are countless small tricks and techniques you can use to accelerate your sales and increase your earnings. The potential is limitless and it's only going to grow as ecommerce becomes more and more widely accepted.

To recap then and to set you off, just follow these simple steps:

#1

Decide what kind of business you will be running. Is this something you're adding to your existing highstreet store? Or are you designing a store to run as a side business while you continue with your current employment?

#2

Choose a type of product, choose a type of niche and choose an audience. Think about how you'll create and procure your products but also think about the amount of competition you'll face and the keyphrases you'll come up against.

#3

Create your website and add an ecommerce platform. Use WordPress and either WooCommerce or Shopify for the majority of scenarios.

#4

Start adding themes and plugins and think about how you're going to layout your site.

#5

Begin marketing your site through social media and with a blog. Reinvest the profits in more stock and more marketing and keep a close eye on what's working!

Rinse and repeat these steps and before you know it, you'll be able to start expanding your operations. Next step: buying your own warehouse!

Printed by Libri Plureos GmbH in Hamburg,
Germany

.